ROY BLATCHFORD

THE
THREE MINUTE
LEADER

First Published 2020

by John Catt Educational Ltd,
15 Riduna Park, Station Road,
Melton, Woodbridge IP12 1QT

Tel: +44 (0) 1394 389850
Email: enquiries@johncatt.com
Website: www.johncatt.com

ISBN: 978 1 912906 90 1

Set and designed by John Catt Educational Limited

INTRODUCTION

By way of a fun bit of light action research, a group of primary and secondary headteacher colleagues set about the following task.

In their very busy, on average, 12 hour days, how many different professional interactions did they have? Conversations – long and short – with children, students, staff, parents, governors, teachers, visitors; emails, messaging, drafting papers, reading reports, phone-calls.

I asked them to take a typical hour and count them all.

The result: 20 an hour – sometimes more, sometimes fewer. That is roughly three minutes per interaction, carried on through breaktime, lunch and snatched cups of tea and coffee during the long working day. An impressive, and sobering, 240 per day!

So the title of this book took shape: *The Three Minute Leader.*

'Less is more' is its guiding principle. The book set outs 101 snippets of advice, provocation and reflection to encourage school leaders as they go about their daily routines. Enjoying and having fun with the role is the key ingredient.

And successful school leaders I know around the globe possess the three essentials of leadership in any context: *humanity, clarity, courage.*

I worked as a young deputy – in a London grammar school going comprehensive – to an experienced headteacher. In my enthusiasm I often challenged him. One day he took me aside and offered this kind observation: 'Roy, you will watch me make mistakes. You will not repeat them. But you will certainly make your own.'

He was right. We are humans, hard-wired to get things right and wrong. Like Scott Fitzgerald's *The Great Gatsby*, we beat on, boats against the current, borne back ceaselessly into our past.

We are also in the people business – and this short compendium is for the good people who are school leaders, wherever on the globe they find themselves.

Roy Blatchford

'To be nobody but yourself in a world which is doing its best night and day to make you like everybody else means to fight the hardest battle which any human being can fight and never stop fighting.'

e.e. cummings

1. 80% OF SUCCESS IS TURNING UP

I once listened to an infamous actor talking about fellow actors arriving late on a movie set. He quipped that 80% of success is turning up. Not a bad adage in some walks of life, but probably not good enough for a leading professional in the public services.

Education leaders must look after their own physical and mental well-being so that they are healthy throughout the year, including during holiday periods. They need to pace themselves and switch off the email sometimes – seriously. Graveyards are full of indispensable people.

Leaders need to be present in their schools most of the time, even when those who deputise are excellent. Visibility counts.

Equally, they make wise judgements as to when they can afford and need to be out of school: presenting, networking, representing, promoting, learning, recruiting. These things matter in the contemporary education landscape.

2. COMPLIMENT SOMEONE AT LEAST ONCE A DAY

Leaders are paid to smile or, as some would describe it, not have a bad hair day. Leaders' enthusiasms, wit, good humour and physical demeanour set the tone.

That means actively communicating with all colleagues in classrooms and laboratories, on corridors, in offices, kitchens and playgrounds.

Compliment those around you when they deserve it. You may find it hard to include all your staff here, but try! Practise on someone who might least expect a smile from you. Offer to take a lesson for them.

In your bleakest moments in a staff meeting, remember: cynics don't only grow old, they die. And that humour is a powerful force.

3. TALK WITH AND LISTEN TO CHILDREN AND STUDENTS

Children help you keep your finger on the school's pulse, its corridor rumours and playground gossip. Walk around classrooms every day you can, even if it's just to say hello and rehearse your vital knowledge of pupils' names. And practise 'hello' in the languages spoken by students.

Students will tell you what's trending on social media, what music to listen to, what films to watch, which teams they and their families support.

You'll also learn what students are enjoying about school, which staff are really exciting them in their learning. If there are occasional undercurrents of disquiet in the community you'll pick these up too.

Hearing can be a passive activity. Listening, with ears and eyes, is active. Practise it.

4. TALK WITH AND LISTEN TO COLLEAGUES

This may be obvious, but where it is more honoured in the breach than the observance you have an unhappy school community.

Leaders listen intently and purposefully to their colleagues. They test the temperature of the organisation through conversations and model a 'without fear or favour' response to simple and difficult questions alike.

Go out of your way to hear from the front-of-house staff; they really know what's occurring.

A number of leaders I know deliberately spend Friday afternoons walking around the school, talking with and listening to colleagues – an optimistic reminder to everyone that all is well in the world and a suitable preparation for the weekend.

And generally work with your office door open. When it's closed colleagues will respect that message and not disturb you.

5. GRASP NETTLES TIGHTLY

A boy brushed a nettle and was stung by it. His mother told him: 'It stung you because you brushed it. Next time grasp it boldly and it will be soft as silk and not hurt you.' Remember Aesop?

Of course, you can be tempted to grasp boldly, overreact and get something wrong. But faced with both tractable and intractable problems, wise leaders recognise the need to resolve matters as speedily and as transparently as possible.

What the leader does, and how they do it, offers a model to others.

Courageous decision making is infectious. And it may, sadly, sometimes cause hurt.

Spot the member of staff who has retired, but hasn't told you. What are you doing to re-energise the person or, frankly, grasp the nettle and say teaching everyday is no longer for him or her?

6. REMEMBER BERTRAND RUSSELL

'The trouble with the world is that the stupid are cocksure and the intelligent are full of doubt.' Thus spake the celebrated philosopher.

Leading a small or large team of professionals, each with their own viewpoints and backgrounds, requires highly tuned antennae. Whose opinions do others on your staff value? Whose do they have less respect for?

In staff meetings, who speaks and who listens? How do you elicit the views of those who are full of doubt? And how do you harness the cocksure in a way that values and moderates their contributions?

Animated debate about education issues is a hallmark of successful schools. White noise and negative gossip should be lanced, promptly.

7. KNOW YOUR COMMUNITY

A hallmark of good leaders – and their senior teams – is that they know in depth their school and local community. They have invested time and research into the people, places and politics which make the school tick.

Astute leaders are smart readers of the rhythms of a school year.

They sense when things are right or wrong, peaceful or disturbed; and, over time, have the uncanny knack of anticipating when trouble is brewing.

If the local community is changing socially and demographically, thoughtful response is required. Nurture community groups.

Don't wait to be told that the number of bilingual learners has doubled since you last looked at the data in September. Or that certain year groups have developed a pattern of students leaving for other schools.

Know the predispositions, prejudices and preferences of those you lead and serve.

8. INVEST IN HIGH QUALITY REFRESHMENTS, TOILETS AND PARKING

The Chief Executive of one of the UK's great tourist attractions says that on feedback surveys, visitors rarely comment on what they have come to see. What they do hold forth on are refreshments, toilets and parking. And, invariably, associated queueing.

Talk to staff, students, parents and governors – and the tale is not dissimilar. In boarding schools, it's food, food and food the students comment on.

In recent years, most schools have transformed refreshments and toilets for staff and students alike. Parking is another matter – you manage the spaces and the access points as best you can. Bikes not cars are the increasing trend, led by climate savvy students.

Remember too the Disney law of queueing: the queue must always be moving; those in line must always be able to see the head of the queue; the queue must be entertained.

9. INVEST IN CLASSROOMS

Teachers and students spend 1,500 hours a year in them. Their well-being and thus their full attendance depend on classrooms being well-lit, airy and of pleasant temperature – wherever in the world.

The air-conditioners in some classrooms drown out voices; think about the importance of acoustics for all students. The heating in some stifles students' thinking – turn it down.

Buy for every classroom a Nespresso machine, a water cooler, a chaise longue: coffee for the teacher, water for the children, and a chaise longue as a reminder that the teacher does not have to stand at the front of a class all the time. S/he can sometimes sit in comfort, listen, and let the students lead learning.

10. ABOLISH BELLS

They belong in another era, an industrial age of clocking on and clocking off. You are not running an assembly line.

Bells at the end of lessons mean lessons 'end' when the bell goes – or rather the flow of important learning is interrupted for students and teachers alike. Homework is set in a rush.

Think differently and give everyone the dignity of managing their time effectively. Everyone has a watch, a phone or a clock they can see.

For emergencies and evacuation – by all means, yes to bells and whistles.

While you're at it, put plants and carpets across the curriculum. In the entrance foyer install: a luxury fish tank to calm irate parents and governors; eye-catching clocks set to different time-zones; and, if space allows, a grand piano as a symbol of musical excellence.

TAKE A BREAK

Perspective

An 18 year-old girl away at boarding school writes to her parents.

Dear Mummy and Daddy

I have to tell you that I have ended up — unexpectedly — in hospital, with both legs broken. I have also fallen in love with an Australian nurse — in fact we are going to get married, emigrate and I am about to have his baby.

None of the above is true, but I have just failed my final exams, and I thought you ought to put things in perspective.

Yours,

Trudy

11. YOUR BEST FRIENDS ARE THE DUSTBIN AND THE DELETE BUTTON

Some headteachers enjoy opening the school's daily postbag so they can delight in binning much of it – a useful therapy. Others ensure a skilled secretary screens out unwanted emails.

Leaders need a device to ensure sanity in a world which threatens to overwhelm with information. And a system which ensures that the important and the urgent are equally weighed.

So much 'stuff' comes your way, so protect others from it. Cut bureaucracy for your colleagues, and they will thank you warmly.

While you're at it: declutter classrooms, offices and staffrooms – secure a deal with a skip company for a weekly recycling collection.

12. BE CONCISE

In the face of daunting bureaucracy, wise leaders know how to cut to the chase.

Emails, reports, letters of complaint, advisory notes, safeguarding updates, board minutes, financial spreadsheets – the sheer volume of material can threaten to swamp.

One hallmark of thoughtful leadership is the ability to sift at pace, with an eye for the important detail.

When writing: craft one side of A4 with the right words in the right order. A single sheet is practical and accessible for any audience whether governor, inspector or parent. Clarity is the watchword.

Less is usually more. On occasion, more is more.

13. BOTTLE THE STAFF WHO ARE YOUNG AT HEART

The young at heart come in all ages and the perceptive leader recognises so.

How many teachers have taught for ten years and made sure that each one of those years has given them something different professionally which has kept them fresh?

Good leaders seek to give all staff the opportunity to stay fresh in the job – and ensure they appoint colleagues with a variety of skills and intelligences. They 'grow' their own great people. They 'coach' at every opportunity.

Infect everyone with the dispositions of the young at heart.

Great teachers remain children at heart, however long they have been in the classroom. Great teachers don't lose their class with age.

14. STICK CLOSE TO YOUR VALUES

'Most of the change we think we see in life is due to truths being in and out of favour.' Poet Robert Frost's words are a reminder that strong school leaders stick to their professional and personal values particularly in times of change.

Your values embody your humanity. Your personal integrity is rooted here.

Thriving on change is what effective leadership is about in the 21st century. Leaders pursuing what they know to be right for their students, staff and school communities is equally vital.

And, occasionally, be sceptical of your values. Talk them through and test them out with trusted colleagues – and maybe with some rogue voices too. Be explicit about the ethical principles upon which you lead.

15. BE CONFIDENT IN YOUR INSTINCTS AND INTUITIONS

People enter teaching and move into leadership positions because they are inspired by a moral commitment to make a difference to young people's lives – and frequently by a real passion for a subject such as geography or mathematics, the joys of which they wish to share with a wider audience.

In any walk of professional life, instinct and intuitions play a key part in how people behave towards others, react to situations, manage challenging moments, and champion achievements.

Having confidence in those instincts and intuitions distinguishes the trusted and creative leader.

'Maverick' can be a maligning word. The dictionary speaks of 'independent minded'. Embrace the mavericks, don't reject them unthinkingly. There is a maverick instinct lurking inside most leaders.

16. ASK SOMEONE TO RESTRAIN YOU

We all need strong supporters in our workplace. Yet someone to restrain you is equally important.

You have been on an exciting overseas visit, listened to an inspiring speaker, watched amazing learning in another school. You return to your setting bursting with ideas and wanting to effect rapid change.

Wise leaders recognise the value of having a deputy who can restrain, not block or hinder. Or a colleague who can listen with integrity, perhaps counsel caution. That *trusted* colleague can come in many guises: a nurse, an IT technician, a member of the administrative staff, a groundsman. They offer the leader space.

Embrace the importance of an everyday sounding-board to challenge kindly your practised ways of thinking and doing.

17. KNOW YOUR SUPPORTERS

'Keep your friends close and your enemies closer' – so runs the Godfather's advice. Experienced leaders know where contrary voices will come from and learn to manage them skilfully, marginalising the destructive and the cynical.

Equally, leaders know that their supporters come in many shapes and sizes – and are a fundamental ingredient in sustaining success.

Children and students are invariably strong ambassadors for their schools, especially in those where their voice is not only heard but listened to. Always let students loose on doubting inspectors – they will never let you down.

Teachers, support staff, governors, parents, local businesses, even the local press – thoughtfully nurtured, these supporters will move your way when you really need them.

18. ENJOY CONFRONTING AUTHORITY

'Confront' is a provocative word. Yet as the leader you may be the only person in the school who is truly in a position to challenge an external pressure or written command.

Personal resilience, sometimes bloody-mindedness, emollience and political guile are required to see off what members of the school community commonly perceive as a threat to its integrity and everyday well-being.

Unreasonable demands for staff to attend external meetings during the school day; requests for data in different formats; school bus companies announcing timetable changes; national guidelines on a political fad – wise leaders can sniff them out and confront the various perpetrators with a smile in their voice.

The Dalai Lama observes: 'Know the rules well, so you can break them properly.'

19. ENJOY TAKING RISKS

In a risk averse age, leaders find it hard to take any enjoyment from risk taking. And contemporary social media make it even more difficult. Yet to fail wisely is at the heart of making progress – excelling at a skill today that a few months previously you had just grasped.

Failure and risk in the classroom, on the sports field, on an outward bound expedition are an integral part of good learning. Teachers give students those opportunities daily, correcting mistakes and applauding achievements.

So too do confident leaders need to enjoy measured risk-taking: with staffing, curriculum, recruitment and retention, CPD, administration, budget setting – all with the aim of enhancing children's schooling.

Children only get one chance, yes. But a school will stand still if leaders are timid and play too safe.

20. PROVIDE STABILITY

It is perhaps of little surprise to read current research that highlights highly successful schools being led by the same principal or headteacher over a lengthy period of time.

In a hurtling, uncertain world, stability at senior level provides students, staff, parents and governors with welcome certainty.

Stability is not stagnation. You can smell that pretty quickly. Rather, there is a culture of quiet optimism, of kindness, confidence in leadership at all levels, organisational routines of high quality – 'we know where we are and where we are going' say all those involved in the school community.

'Nudge' weighed adroitly with 'direction' is the modus operandi.

TAKE A BREAK

Less is more

- The Lord's Prayer – 54 words.
- The Ten Commandments – 297 words.
- The American Declaration of Independence – 300 words.
- The EEC Directive for exporting duck eggs – 26,911 words.

****

- An ounce of information is worth a pound of data
- An ounce of knowledge is worth a pound of information
- An ounce of understanding is worth a pound of knowledge
- An ounce of wisdom is worth a pound of understanding.

21. IT'S EASIER TO BEG FORGIVENESS THAN SEEK PERMISSION

Not everyone subscribes to this principle of management.

But show me an excellent school leader who seeks permission rather than following deep professional instincts, and I'll show you a school which risks faltering.

Children get one chance at an education, so no leader compromises that basic tenet.

Principled and values-led decision making by senior leadership teams, inclusive of staff and students, creates vibrant teaching and learning communities.

Folk don't look over their shoulders and seek permission. They do occasionally have to say sorry.

22. THRIVE ON ACCOUNTABILITY

And live with occasional chaos. To err is to be human.

Call to mind the old maxim (misquoting Rudyard Kipling): if you have kept your head when everyone around you is losing theirs, you probably haven't quite understood what's going on.

In fact, colleagues are expecting you to be the one who keeps his/her head, particularly when the school is being held to account – when external tests and examination results are being published, when the inspectorate call by. Or when the auditor and health and safety inspector arrive on the same day.

At critical moments like these, effective leaders step up and field with aplomb, dignity and deftness whatever is being said about the school in the public domain. Enjoy the moments!

23. KEEP IN MIND THE BIG PICTURE

Somebody has to.

The helter-skelter of daily routines can be all-consuming for leaders. Some days there has to be the acceptance that it is the regular diurnal round, the sustaining of the status quo, the living with things not being perfect that is good enough.

When organisations hit bumps in the road – as all do from time to time – leaders have to enable their colleagues to keep in mind that bigger picture: what do we stand for as a school, in all its richness?

In holding the wider landscape constantly in their minds, leaders are able to navigate days, weeks, terms and school years with personal and professional confidence.

Lift your eyes to the horizon. Think 'landscape' not 'portrait'.

24. COMMUNICATE, COMMUNICATE, COMMUNICATE

It was the British Prime Minister Tony Blair who used the mantra 'Education, Education, Education' to help win an election. And even his critics would agree that he was a persuasive communicator.

As in parliamentary politics, so in educational leadership. Timing is all. Time your communications well. Repeat the same message several times: staff briefing, tweet, email, assembly.

Have something of merit to say or write. This is not easy week-in-week-out. But those you lead expect it of you. Some heads write a personal weekly bulletin – once begun, it has to be sustained.

How you say something is as important as *what* you say.

It's a truism in the workplace that if colleagues disagree with you they'll be tempted to say you haven't been communicating properly. If you know you have communicated well, hold your ground.

25. TELL COMPELLING STORIES

Leaders in any sphere are usually competent story-tellers. They paint pictures of a better tomorrow. History shows us that great leaders have enjoyed their ability to deliver compelling narratives, for good and ill.

Effective school leaders are equally practised in composing and presenting memorable stories: to students, staff, parents, governors, other stakeholders – and anyone else who is good enough to listen.

Stories may cover quite prosaic topics: why the duty rota needs amending. Or cover significant changes: the school is changing its name, increasing its intake, assuming responsibility for another school, opening an annex in another town!

Whatever the topic, hours spent by leaders preparing and rehearsing the story is time handsomely well spent.

Whether nudging or instructing: 'Thou shall not' might reach the head but it takes 'once upon a time' to reach the heart.

26. HAVE FUN WITH NUMBERS

They say that when you're a hammer everything looks like a nail. Many people enjoy playing and working with numbers more than they do with words. Some staff love data in any form.

School leaders need to recognise that and model their own facility and enjoyment with data – even if it doesn't come naturally.

In a data-rich world, leaders demonstrate that spreadsheets can be a force for good in analysing current achievements *and* pointing new ways forward.

Lies, damn lies and statistics is one state of mind. Another is that fun and creativity with numbers can be infectious.

The Fibonacci series is a good place to start.

27. KEEP THE MAIN THING THE MAIN THING

I have heard political leaders say that you cannot have the word 'priority' in the plural. It's a statement to reflect on. Does your school have too many 'priorities'? Do staff *think* you have?

Wise school leaders may well present a number of priorities for the academic year, but they ensure first that there is sufficient capacity to follow through on those priorities.

If leaders don't offer focus, and begin to wander from their intended path, staff will wander too. Energies will be dissipated, morale weakened, whole-staff commitment to the cause dented. And students will sense it.

Reassure yourself that no organisation can do everything it wants to, all of the time.

28. DON'T ASSUME RATIONALITY ON THE PART OF THE FOLK YOU ARE DEALING WITH

The Chinese/Indian/Arabic proverbs have it that when the winds of change blow, some build walls while others build windmills – a universal theme.

Sustainable change takes time to prepare for; in turn, those affected by the change need time to digest its implications. Thoughtful leaders understand this and orchestrate matters accordingly.

We are irrational and rational beings, sometimes both at the same time. And, backs against the wall, we can overreact against change. 'Doing with' rather than 'doing to' is easy to say, not always easy in practice. *Perception* matters.

Accept the idea that there are multiple perceptions of every situation. And learn to forgive and forget.

29. SPARE A THOUGHT FOR BLOOM

- Synthesis
- Evaluation
- Analysis
- Application
- Comprehension
- Knowledge

An oft-quoted ladder in learning and curriculum progression. If you find Bloom's taxonomy a useful sequential checklist, remember that not everyone is as capable as you might pretend to be of moving upwards through these ways of thinking.

Some staff you work with will genuinely get stuck half-way. Some may deliberately get stuck. Your role – with tact and patience, kindness and a smile – is to help colleagues take the extra steps.

Students familiar with the model might even help the staff's appreciation of Bloom!

30. SPARE A THOUGHT FOR ROUSSEAU

Why? Ethical leadership matters.

A significant influence on the European Enlightenment, the 18th century French philosopher Rousseau placed a sense of self, morality, pity and imagination at the heart of being human.

That sure sense of self, keen self-awareness, clear morality lie deep in good leaders. In turn, they model these qualities to their colleagues.

'Lawyers were children once' wrote the novelist Harper Lee. School leaders remind staff and students of this line – we learn from one another daily as part of our humanity.

You might have other philosophers whose work you like to share with colleagues – don't be shy to do so. Reveal your sources and influencers, as appropriate.

TAKE A BREAK

Teamwork

There are four people named Everybody, Somebody, Anybody and Nobody.

There was an important job to be done and Everybody was asked to do it. Everybody was sure Somebody would do it.

Anybody could have done it, but Nobody did it.

Somebody got angry about that, because it was Everybody's job.

Everybody thought Anybody could do it but Nobody realised that Everybody wouldn't do it.

It ended up that Everybody blamed Somebody when Nobody did what Anybody could have done.

31. AVOID DELUSIONS OF GRANDEUR

The proverbial saying 'power corrupts; absolute power corrupts absolutely' conveys the view that, as a person's power increases, their moral sense diminishes.

There are certainly *rare* cases in schools where headteachers and principals have lost their moral compass and become self-serving. Motivation has turned from doing the best for children to doing the best for themselves, often financially. The media are then merciless.

The overwhelming majority of school leaders rightly see themselves as *primus inter pares*, demonstrating that unfailingly to all stakeholders.

Just occasionally, pause for a moment, rid yourself of any whiff of grandeur. Don't allow ego to trump generosity towards others.

Keep enjoying being the principled leader.

32. READ SENECA AND THE STOICS

Current thinking around ethical leadership in headship partially has its roots in 3rd century BC Athens. The philosophy of Seneca and compatriots asserts that virtue – such as wisdom – is happiness, and judgement should be based on behaviour rather than words.

The Stoics asserted that we don't control and cannot rely on external events, only on ourselves and our responses. That's being stoical.

In an unpredictable world, with humans having but brief lives, the message is: be in control of yourself at least.

Act on what can be acted upon. Don't fret over endless debate.

And when the s**t hits the fan, take the rap. Don't blame others.

33. 'BEING' AND 'DOING'

We are human be-ings before we are human do-ings.

The relentlessness and sometimes loneliness of leading a school is not to be underestimated. Those new to headship often say that it wasn't until they became the leader that they realised this. As a deputy it was different; you were not the final arbiter.

Schools are places where everybody is doing, everybody is busy – except for the handful of students, occasionally staff, who lead a quieter life.....

Leaders get caught up with the completion of to-do lists. If they are not careful, there is no escape.

Listen to some music in your office. Walk outdoors daily. Nurture your inner sloth.

Seize the moment to just stand and stare. To be. You'll be amazed what you sense.

34. LEAVE THEM WITH A SMILE ON THEIR FACE

Leading schools requires taking important decisions at regular intervals. Getting the right *tone* with colleagues matters, especially when difficult messages have to be conveyed.

There is a real knack to 'telling it like it is', and still leaving the member of staff in good spirits.

Accomplished leaders manage to get this right most of the time. And learn quickly when they make a mistake. They remind themselves that: 'It's not what I'm saying that matters. It's what you're hearing'.

As we learnt in high school, according to Marshall McLuhan, *the medium is the message.*

35. IT'S NOT WHAT'S IN THE DIARY THAT KILLS YOU, IT'S WHAT'S NOT IN THE DIARY

Leaders' diaries can be proverbial bomb-sites. Everyone wants to see the leader, right now. But with a full list of scheduled diary commitments, along comes something *really* urgent.

The best school leaders have developed creative solutions to potential diary clashes, usually involving a skilled secretary, willing and well briefed deputies – and the occasional 'white lies'.

Walking the school to hold a few 'must-have conversations' with colleagues is one way to reduce the backlog.

Time juggling is a vital part of the job: live to fight another day. Try to keep 20% of your paper/electronic diary pages blank – they won't stay that way.

If you're not careful, you find you haven't time for what matters most, personally and professionally.

36. LEADERS ENABLE ... MANAGERS CONTROL

It is a natural inclination early in a manager's career to want to control. You've been promoted so show what you can do. Observing skilled middle managers is to see them starting 'tight' then being willing to 'loosen'.

It's certainly what accomplished leaders do: appoint the right people in the right places, and let them flourish in a climate of measured risk.

The average manager seeks to control colleagues, while the confident leader is quite content for others to shine and to take the plaudits.

Appoint good managers and grow great leaders. Let go! Roots and wings are what we give to children and adults alike.

37. TWITTER, ETC.

'It takes a village to raise a child' runs the African proverb. That village in the 21st century has gone global and instant.

Contemporary leadership is played out against a backcloth of 24-hour media, Twitter, Instagram and TikTok. A dance created in Shanghai on a Wednesday is acted out by 10,000 followers on Thursday in Seattle.

Through social media, pupils and parents can turn a petty drama into a crisis at the flick of a thumb.

And leaders need resilience and mutual support when confronted by some of the worst online slanders in local communities.

Headteachers today spend a disproportionate amount of time picking up the pieces of poorly worded emails sent in haste by staff. Astute leaders have established clear protocols for all staff when dealing with social media.

Caveat emptor has become *sender beware*.

38. A QUICK 'NO' OR A SLOW 'YES'

The old adage of 'never say yes in a corridor' rings true for many school leaders. Staff often want instant decisions from leaders – and there's a place for those, for example in certain health and safety contexts.

Wisdom suggests that a little time pondering with colleagues will lead to a better course of actions. Judicious timing in leadership is crucial, so better a quick 'no' and a slow 'yes'.

The alternative can be 'command and reverse', a recipe for confusion.

Recognise the days when your own emotions and state of mind are not at their fittest – that's not a day for major decisions. A reliable PA will tell you which days those are.

39. 'YOU WON'T MAKE MY MISTAKES, YOU'LL MAKE YOUR OWN'

Just about every headteacher can recount tales of how they watched leaders they previously worked with make mistakes. The inner voice says: 'I won't repeat that'. Maybe, maybe not.

Learning from our own mistakes and the errors of others is part of the human condition. Learning how to avoid the same mistakes is the key. And still we fail.

Admitting to mistakes, explaining what went wrong and why, mitigating the consequences – these are what matter in a healthy collegiate context which will understand and forgive. Rely on your senior team to sometimes rescue you.

We must learn to see the world through others' eyes. We often don't and are the poorer for it.

40. BE RESILIENT IN THE FACE OF FAILURE

To be nobody but yourself in a world which is doing its best night and day to make you like everybody else means to fight the hardest battle which any human being can fight and never stop fighting.

e. e. cummings

Leaders in the public services are often under great pressure to perform to externally set targets. There is a parallel pressure to do things in a particular way, to follow the latest orthodoxy in order to achieve the targets.

We cannot succeed all of the time, that is not the human lot. Failure comes, it is said, to make us stronger next time.

Resilience is a buzz word in students' learning today. Leaders and their staff require it too, and may well need help from different sources to build sustained resilience.

TAKE A BREAK

Communication

Head to Deputy: Tomorrow morning there will be an eclipse of the sun at 9am. This is something we can't see every day. Let the pupils line up outside in their best clothes to watch. To mark the occurrence of this rare phenomenon I will personally explain it to them. If it is raining we shall not be able to see it very well and so the pupils should assemble in the hall.

Deputy Head to Senior Teacher: By order of the Head there will be a total eclipse of the sun at 9am tomorrow. If it is raining we shall not be able to see very well on sight, in our best clothes. In that case the disappearance of the sun will be followed through in the hall. This is something that we can't see happen every day.

Senior Teacher to Head of Year: By order of the head we shall follow through, in best clothes, the disappearance of the sun in the hall tomorrow morning at 9am. The Head will tell us whether it is going to rain. This is something we can't see happen every day.

Head of Year to Form Tutor: If it is raining in the hall tomorrow morning, which is something we can't see happen every day, the Head – in her best clothes – will disappear at 9am.

Form Tutor to Pupils: Tomorrow at 9am the Head will disappear. It is a pity that we cannot see this happen every day.

41. TOMORROW WE WILL RUN FASTER

Gatsby believed in the green light, the orgiastic future that year by year recedes before us. It eluded us then, but that's no matter – tomorrow we will run faster, stretch out our arms farther…..And one fine morning -

Author Scott Fitzgerald created the great Jay Gatsby who believed that tomorrow would be better than today. Leaders in public services hold to the same optimistic mantra.

They believe that everyone is interested in doing what they do today a little better than they did it yesterday: staff and students equally.

We need the equivalent of the green light in schools, even though we know in our hearts it may never be reached.

42. LEARN TO LIVE WITHOUT THANKS

As a school leader you will spend much of your time acknowledging and appreciating the work of others – in many ways the heart and pleasure of the job.

If you've worked with good leaders over the years, you will have been motivated by their recognition of your efforts.

Will you be thanked as a leader? Yes, sometimes. Thoughtful and kind chairs of governing boards play that role.

Talk to many headteachers and they affirm that the day they were really thanked was their final day at work – before they departed the school for new opportunities.

Then the appreciation floodgates opened, thanks and gifts were profuse – and they came to realise that they might be missed.

43. THE NOBLE PROFESSION OF TEACHING

Historically, there were said to be three 'noble' professions, which meant they were jobs for people who did not want to sweat: clergymen, lawyers and medical doctors.

That was then. In today's world we would say that most professionals sweat a little.

School leaders – from their own career – know that teaching is a noble and honourable profession in the 21st century. Too often it is not recognised as such. Yet without teaching, societies return to barbarism.

Headteachers and principals play a decisive role in celebrating the high value of the teacher in today's society – in promoting the ethic of public service.

If you don't do it, at every public opportunity, who will?

44. 'WE' NOT 'I'

'A leader is best when the people barely know he exists. When his work is done, his aim fulfilled, they will say: we did it ourselves.'

So run the words of Chinese philosopher Lao Tzu. Contexts and cultures are different and various, yet some truisms cross boundaries.

For the school leader, the cultivating of 'we' not 'I' is pivotal to sustaining a vibrant and forward-thinking school community. It's not easy to achieve, that balance between *showing* and *sharing* the way ahead – and wisely knowing when to step back.

Language is key, both spoken and written.

Beware the headteacher who talks about *my* school.

45. A SENSE OF URGENCY AT THE RIGHT TIME

You set the pace of the school you lead. Those schools where the headteacher is 'on it' have a can-do atmosphere that is palpable. And it's not difficult to sniff the complacent, laissez-faire opposite.

Skilful orchestration of the pace at which a school community moves ahead lies at the core of informed leadership.

That means not placing undue pressures on staff and students. It can also mean that the school can adopt a sense of urgency when it's needed at certain points.

You will make the fine call as to when, and for how long, your school can shift gear in the best interests of students and staff. Seize the opportunity when it presents itself.

46. IT'S NEVER TOO LATE

In tandem with 'a sense of urgency at the right time', the wisely restless school adopts a proper approach to change.

Not change for change sake – but when something arises that you identify needs prompt action, you don't wait for the new term or the new school year. You act now.

You persuade colleagues of the imperative of a timely response. You discuss with relevant staff, you think through unintended consequences, you communicate thoughtfully to all stakeholders, you decide.

Act in haste and repent at leisure is the cautionary warning. But you know that time is precious in a child's school life – and you back your judgements.

Always remember that the standards you walk past are the standards you accept.

47. NO SURPRISES

On a personal level, most (not all) of us like surprises from time to time: bumping into old friends, receiving gifts, hearing from family members.

But surprises in a professional context are not usually welcome. Indeed the 'policy and practice of no surprises' appears as a mantra in most management and leadership training. 'Surprise' takes on a negative connotation.

School leaders need to be *clear* with colleagues what is meant by 'no surprises'. One person's interpretation and appreciation may not be the same as another's, personally or professionally.

Describe to colleagues what you mean by the phrase, then they won't surprise you unpleasantly. And always welcome the pleasant surprise.

48. 'LET'S ALL HAVE A GOOD YEAR AT THE SAME TIME'

Faced with variable performance data in the summer GCSE examinations, one headteacher began his September staff meeting with the words: 'Let's all have a good year at the same time'.

If only! Easier said than done.

Ambitious leaders take the greatest enjoyment from, and see their purpose in creating an optimistic working environment where all colleagues can thrive in good spirits.

Yet in the course of a school year, events intervene and lead to variability: illness, family bereavement, accidents and incidents – for students and staff alike.

Living with and managing 'stuff happening' is the leader's reality. Prepare yourself as best you can – if the budget allows, appoint some reserves.

49. THE FUN AND FUNDAMENTALS

Effective learning of any new piece of knowledge or range of skills requires both the fun and the fundamentals.

If learning has no fun about it, there is little motivation for the learner. If the learner doesn't practise and dedicate time, then progress will be slow.

Leadership in schools is no different. Leaders seek to enable staff and students to have fun, be playful and enjoy their work – at the same time expecting the fundamentals of organisational discipline, routines and expectations to operate consistently.

The fun and fundamentals cocktail is a winning one in any workplace – and is a language readily remembered and understood. 'Fun' and 'mental' in the words of one witty eight year old!

50. JUDGEMENT OR LUCK

What does it take to make good judgements?

Feel, intuition, hunch, faith, knowledge, wisdom, advice, experience – or is it luck?

- The million dollar deal-maker says 'luck is what happens when preparation meets opportunity.'
- The sports champion says 'the more I practise the luckier I get.'
- The chancer says 'luck is what happens to me that is outside my control.'

In politics, it is hearts, minds, communication, timing…. and luck which determine failure or success. So in school leadership.

Rely on your good judgement. Don't underestimate luck.

TAKE A BREAK

Certainty

Two battleships assigned to the training squadron had been at sea on manoeuvres in heavy weather for several days. I was serving on the lead battleship and was on watch on the bridge as night fell.

The visibility was poor with patchy fog, so the captain remained on the bridge keeping an eye on all activities.

Shortly after dark, the lookout on the wing of the bridge reported, 'Light, bearing on the starboard bow.'

'Is it steady or moving astern?' the captain called out.

Lookout replied, 'Steady, captain,' which meant we were on a dangerous collision course with that ship.

The captain then called to the signalman, 'Signal that ship: we are on a collision course, advise you change course 20 degrees.'

Back came a signal, 'Advisable for you to change course 20 degrees.'

The captain said, 'Send, I'm a captain, change course 20 degrees.'

'I'm a seaman second class,' came the reply. 'You had better change course 20 degrees.'

By that time, the captain was furious. He spat out, 'Send, I'm a battleship. Change course 20 degrees.'

Back came the flashing light, 'I'm a lighthouse.'

We changed course.

51. VALUE CRITICAL VOICES

They f*** you up, your mum and dad.
They may not mean to, but they do.
They fill you with the faults they had
And add some extra, just for you.

Poet Philip Larkin's infamous lines about parents provide a prompt that truth to power is a pre-requisite for successful leadership in any business.

Listening to critical voices, wherever they come from, strengthens an organisation, once the leaders have digested and reflected on what the voices have to say.

Collusion and patience with unacceptable practices drag down any organisation. An open ear to critique is invaluable, leading to a 'no excuses' culture.

Listen to what students, staff, the complaining customers have to say.

'The customer is not always right,' adds the wise leader.

52. BLINK

Blink. Life goes faster than you think. A school year can gallop away and you've not found time to step back and take stock of strengths and weaknesses. What's happening that I have missed? Where is credit due and I have failed to offer it?

A formal external inspection may have given you some timely pointers. But enterprising leaders invite an outside pair of eyes *every* year to help them see the school afresh.

Napoleon possessed 'le coup d'oeil' – the glance.

Experienced headteachers/principals from another context can offer valuable insights into the classrooms, the corridors, the systems. Ask them to observe sharply.

Invite a trusted source to come and *Blink* with you.

53. TIGHTEN UP TO BE GOOD, LOOSEN TO BE EXCELLENT

Experienced leaders understand this idea. Inexperienced ones can get it wrong.

On a school improvement journey, tighten up the systems and the expectations – and good provision will be realised.

On the journey to excellence, by all means 'loosen' – but don't stop tightening. It's not an either/or.

Choose carefully which aspects of the organisation can be loosened, or the previous gains will be compromised.

It's a mantra that works, when accompanied by precision and watchfulness.

Go visit someone else who has tried the model before letting it loose in your own context.

54. WITHOUT A VISION, THE PEOPLE PERISH

Featured in a number of religious texts is the exhortation that the people perish where there is no vision.

A ubiquitous feature of great schools across the world is their clarity of vision: a set of aims and goals underpinned by values which are crisply stated, widely shared and understood by all who make up the school community.

In turn, those who lead these schools are able to articulate skilfully, for different audiences, what the vision means in the day-to-day of students' lives.

Education leaders spend time shaping, articulating, refining their visions.

Take pride in and enjoy this seminal aspect of your role.

55. LEAN IN

Sheryl Sandberg, Facebook Chief Operating Officer, wrote a book of this title urging women leaders to 'Believe in yourself – lean in!' and 'Find something you love doing, and do it with gusto'.

Her messages to women and men alike are worth reading in the original. Ms Sandberg has sustained her global leadership role.

Accomplished school leaders focus inwards into their organisations, tackle the thorny issues with integrity, bring emotional and physical energy, encourage others not to fear failure. They delegate carefully and genuinely.

As you lean in and focus on what matters everyday, colleagues value your commitment and dedication – and are motivated by it. They know you care.

56. LEAN OUT

If as a leader you are going to continue to paint pictures of a better tomorrow, go visit a few galleries: education and commercial settings where leaders are doing cutting-edge things.

Go see what another school, in another part of the country, is achieving with a school population akin to yours – and visit one that is very different. Visit an HR department in a local big business.

School leaders often return to their own setting with renewed confidence in their own practices. Just sometimes they return and nuance their home systems.

Enable your colleagues to do the same: to be inspired by a fellow professional outside their usual setting – and, equally important, to return having had their everyday practices affirmed.

57. IF YOU STAND STILL LONG ENOUGH YOU BECOME A RADICAL

At a retirement event I heard a headteacher of 20 years standing observe that his educational philosophies had been in and out of favour at least three times in that period.

Successful leaders nuance school practices to keep them fresh and reflective of emerging research evidence or social change. Equally they hold dear to what they know is professionally right for the community they serve.

They are not fearful of acknowledging then ignoring the latest political fashion. They serve without fear or favour, confident that educational outcomes for their young people are the best they can be.

These successful leaders are not complacent or arrogant. Their focus is ensuring all students leave school with dignity and self-worth.

58. GETTING IT RIGHT, NOT BEING RIGHT

'Some are born great, some achieve greatness, and some have greatness thrust upon them'. Thus Shakespeare in *Twelfth Night*.

We are no longer in an age of the divine right of kings and queens. 'Getting things right' as a leader matters very much – and more than the leader 'being right'.

Of course personal pride comes into play. You've argued for a good while that a certain way of teaching, pupil grouping, staff structuring or timetabling is the right way – and thus over time it has proved. You keep that inner pride humbly to yourself – let others applaud or take credit as they wish.

What matters for the children and the students is that the way in which the school is working is more than fit for purpose.

59. VALUE ADDED.....VALUES ADDED

'Si monumentum requiris, circumspice – if you seek his monument, look around.' (Epitaph of Sir Christopher Wren, architect of St Paul's Cathedral, London.)

Look around the school you lead. Are values added and value added equally weighed in practice?

Big data and small data dominate personal and professional worlds. Every school has its data specialists, or it would be nowhere. And where does precision data lead? It leads to the notion of *value* added.

We invest this much expenditure, teacher resource, student support – and we can see, over time, what measured value (progress, achievement) the school has added for its students. That's OK as far as it goes.

The smart leader says that just as important are *values* added. How is what the school is doing adding to the life experiences of a child, broadening her/his horizons, helping them understand local and global issues?

60. IT'S THE CLASSROOM, STUPID

US President Bill Clinton famously won office with the campaign slogan 'It's the economy, stupid.'

Successful principals and headteachers across the world know that what goes on in classrooms lies at the very heart of their business. And they have a first-class command of what is happening in those classrooms.

They know the sparkling cocktail: attractive and spacious environments; excellent resources; well planned, knowledgeable, motivational teaching; children engaged in rich tasks; teachers and students together identifying what makes for good progress and effective next steps in learning; meaningful home-study tasks.

Confident leaders have created a culture where teachers teach with the door open, so best practices are shared without fuss.

What's the picture from where you stand? Do you really *know* your classrooms?

TAKE A BREAK

Mcnamara fallacy

The first step is to measure whatever can be easily measured. This is OK as far as it goes.

The second step is to disregard that which can't be easily measured or to give it an arbitrary quantitative value. This is artificial and misleading.

The third step is to presume that what can't be measured easily really isn't important. This is blindness.

The fourth step is to say that what can't be easily measured really doesn't exist. This is suicide.

61. GIVE YOURSELF A BACK DOOR

I worked once with a chair of governors of wonderful contradictions: quirky and safe, irreverent and wise, wry and expansive. He was full of well judged *bons mots*.

Faced with a potentially difficult audience, he would always ask where the back door was. His command of metaphor was fascinating.

School leaders know that the proverbial back door can be a face saver, an essential in management as the need arises. What are your 'back door' techniques?

When making major announcements, pause to think through the unintended consequences. And just maybe have an alternative or two up your sleeve.

Spend an away-day with the senior team rehearsing, anticipating, analysing: How Projects Fail. Time well spent on any leadership journey.

62. POSTCARDS AND PRAISE

Thanking and rewarding colleagues in the workplace is a natural and pleasurable activity for leaders. Getting the tone and the practicalities right, week in and week out, can be a challenge.

How do you judge just how many thank-you postcards a week, a term to give to staff? Is an email worth sending, and is it valued?

'Praise where praise is due' – as with children and students – is a useful guide. Don't underestimate the motivational power of good words for good deeds.

And as a school leader doubtless used to receiving complaints, make sure there is a Compliments Book in the entrance foyer in which departing visitors can write nice things, just as fine hotels have.

63. ASSEMBLIES

Assemblies, meditations, thoughts for the day – they come in many forms and remain a fixture in schools. We need to make the most of them, given the time they consume over an academic year.

Begin an assembly with something playful: 'The culture of Romanticism has it that 2 + 2 = 4 ½, and that's near enough.'

Assemblies are often a judicious mix of *worship* and *worthship*. Importantly, they afford an opportunity to celebrate the breadth of achievements by students each and every day.

They are a reminder of students' duty and commitment to one another as learners and young citizens. And of the whole school being the sum of its diverse parts.

Student-led or teacher-led assemblies? Which are yours? Where does the best balance lie?

64. EVERYONE'S WATCHING YOU

School leaders are certainly watched in assemblies, often by parents and visitors, for how they model the craft of teaching.

You are never off duty, especially in a boarding school context.

Your spoken language, body language, interpersonal skills, personal interests, professional prejudices, office decor and artefacts – staff are always watching your actions and weighing your words.

Leaders at ease with themselves and comfortable in their own skin command respect and are often major influencers in staff's lives. Just ask headteachers about conversations – and letters received – they have enjoyed later in life with former colleagues.

You do what comes naturally to you. There are occasions when you have to resist – with tact – how others choose to see you and interpret your words.

65. ATTENTION TO DETAIL

Political biographies are replete with British Cabinet members' stories about their famous red boxes being left on buses and trains. They also testify that one politician's attention to detail is not another's – in terms of depth, care, accuracy and regularity.

The school leader has the equivalent of the red box in their daily in-tray, electronic and on paper. Time has to be found to deal with the detail; on occasion that detail can be thoughtfully delegated.

Attention to detail matters in the people business: responding to the needs of colleagues and students, and, crucially, following up where required with reports, letters, phone-calls, referrals.

'The devil is in the detail' – it so often is. In matters such as safeguarding, examination entries, qualification checks, experienced heads know where the pitfalls lie.

Ensure you have someone in your lead administrative team whose eye for the right detail is sharp. That will save you angst and time.

66. TIME

Time present and time past
Are both perhaps present in time future.
And time future contained in time past.

T.S. Eliot

She who writes the timetable is the mistress of time. There can be no more important task in a school than carving out the lives of hundreds or thousands of adults and young people for a whole year.

The productive use of time is what all leaders want to see each day, each week. There is no better way of judging a vibrant school than to watch how staff and students move with purpose at transition times, within and outside lessons. It speaks volumes.

Leaders know this to be true and model the way.

Giving time to colleagues and students is the greatest gift you can give in a hurried world.

67. INNOVATE

Author William Gibson wryly noted that the future is already here, but it's just not very evenly distributed.

One person's innovation is another person's established practice.

It's a *culture* of innovative thinking and doing that characterises the practice of excellent leaders. Thus staff are stimulated to look afresh at how students learn in school and at home. They try different ways of teaching a familiar topic, harnessing out-of-the-box resources on-line and in print.

Leaders of special schools are particularly adept at innovative teaching techniques, seeking to find different ways of enabling students with physical and cognitive difficulties to access knowledge and life-skills.

What's the climate for innovation in your school context?

68. CURRICULUM VOICES

Does it matter what we teach? There are many voices, views and templates.

In essence, a country's history, traditions and values lie at the heart of a given national curriculum. Additionally, the curriculum is preparing students with the knowledge and skills required for today's and tomorrow's global society.

There's some guesswork about the future of course.

Open leadership enables groups of teachers to plan and play with ideas together – to harness their own passions and knowledge into learning plans that will intrigue and motivate children.

You know as a confident leader that the blending of tried and tested topics with techniques, technologies and subject matter which anticipate the future – that's what makes for a memorable curriculum.

69. CULTURE TRUMPS SYSTEMS

'Culture eats strategy for breakfast', proclaimed management guru Peter Drucker.

School leaders who work or have worked in different parts of the world will at once testify to the fact that culture trumps systems.

You may have a practised way of appointing staff, conducting health and safety reviews, reporting to parents – each in turn is trumped by local rules and regulations, and cultural sensitivities. You will need to adapt. Assuredly, the National Ministry will come to inspect.

Closer to home, leaders who have taken on schools with entrenched and failing ways of doing will know that culture strangles progress if you're not agile, persistent and insistent that change must come.

Look at the pervading culture of your own setting. Does it ever risk cramping individual enterprise?

70. BUT SYSTEMS MATTER

'Everything in its place and a place for everything' might be a fair description of a school where systems are tight, fit for purpose and enabling.

Like a finely tuned Mercedes, this does not happen by chance. Smart design has created the system; good brains have fine-tuned it; the system constantly puts the users first.

Proven, refined, updated systems across a school make daily routines workable and apparently effortless. In common with the best sports referees whom you don't see in the game, the systems are quietly unseen and instil confidence.

And emergencies don't catch anyone out. Responses have been exhaustively rehearsed.

Don't underplay – nor under-resource – the magic of great systems. Look at the clutter of certain school websites to see where whole-school systems are ailing.

TAKE A BREAK

The seven principles of public life

These were first set out by Lord Nolan in 1995 and are included in the Ministerial code.

- *Selflessness*: Holders of public office should act solely in terms of the public interest.

- *Integrity*: Holders of public office must avoid placing themselves under any obligation to people or organisations that might try inappropriately to influence them in their work. They should not act or take decisions in order to gain financial or other material benefits themselves, their family, or their friends. They must declare and resolve any interests and relationships.

- *Objectivity*: Holders of public office must act and take decisions impartially, fairly and on merit, using the best evidence and without discrimination or bias.

- *Accountability*: Holders of public office are accountable to the public for their decisions and actions and must submit themselves to the scrutiny necessary to ensure this.

- *Openness*: Holders of public office should act and take decisions in an open and transparent manner. Information should not be withheld from the public unless there are clear and lawful reasons for so doing.

- *Honesty*: Holders of public office should be truthful.

- *Leadership*: Holders of public office should exhibit these principles in their own behaviour. They should actively promote and robustly support the principles and be willing to challenge poor behaviour wherever it occurs.

71. LEAD FROM THE FRONT

Everything has been said before. The challenge is to think of it again.
Goethe

Everything has been said. But not everyone has yet said it.
Chief Rabbi

These trenchant observations from different sources are a reminder to leaders that it's not easy to be original but that people need energising to tackle contemporary challenges.

Leading from the front is not about being a hero/heroine innovator, a gifted orator, nor a Renaissance thinker. While there are some generic qualities and skills in all leaders, each is her/his own person.

- Be well organised, but not intimidatingly so.
- Show empathy, sympathy and humility where appropriate.
- Present an attitude of mind that is open to others' thoughts and ideas.
- Be consistent in words and deeds.
- Don't be too serious or earnest.

Even try cultivating a few weaknesses to match your natural ones! Deputies can usually help you here.

72. LEAD FROM BEHIND

Experienced leaders can play various roles if they choose to delegate effectively and find time for leading from behind.

- You are a teacher, with proven expertise, so quietly help others to correct their mistakes.
- Coach those middle leaders in the leadership traits you know work and will suit them as individuals.
- Invest in developing your senior team, to whom you owe so much.
- Give time generously to those on your staff who most need it at a particular period in their work.
- Offer to do some background research or writing lesson materials.

And if you're going to work until 70+, move to four days a week for a year, set up a co-headship, or have a sabbatical.

73. INTELLECTUAL LEADERSHIP

You likely entered the profession as a well educated person in your own right, probably with a passion for a subject. You may view teaching as a vocation – duty has called. You may have a hinterland in a different profession or context.

School leaders are frequently recognised for their own scholarship and great subject knowledge, whether they currently teach a class or not. It is important that colleagues know what you can teach with expertise.

The leader is not expected to be a polymath. But you should inspire others – by example – to read, research, publish and lecture. You should prompt teachers, administrators, technicians, support staff to broaden their own intellectual horizons.

There is a palpable buzz in staffrooms where colleagues share recent research in their subject or about the craft of the classroom.

What's been your latest nudge to staff in this arena?

74. APPOINT COLLEAGUES SMARTER THAN YOU ARE

There's a fascinating book titled *Are you smart enough to work at Google?* which outlines how the $1 trillion global company appoints people. Naturally, they want smart staff.

But there's no reason why schools shouldn't attract the best brains with great interpersonal skills and a vocation to work with children

Skilled school leaders study CVs to see what range of skills, interests and experiences new appointments will bring to the staffroom. Brave leaders will not be nervous about securing the talents of those with much higher grades than the leader has.

'Do not confine your children to your own learning for they were born in a different time', runs the sage Hebrew proverb.

75. CAREFUL

You watch some people – and they are naturally careful. You visit some schools and you detect at once that they are careful by design and intent.

- Careful with the way you have been received over the phone in arranging the visit and on arrival at the 'Press Here' gates/doors.
- Careful with how you are welcomed and seated in an attractive reception area.
- Careful with how staff and students greet and pass each other as they move around the building.
- Careful with fresh displays in the corridors and common spaces.
- Careful with lunch and break arrangements, providing adequate seating for children.
- Careful with your visit in all respects.

You'd like to visit again, bringing some colleagues to see and feel a school at ease with itself.

76. CARELESS

You watch some people – and they are just careless. You visit some schools and their carelessness is professionally depressing.

- The environment, from the reception area to the dining hall, is scruffy and neglected. It requires a deep clean.
- Students and staff do not interact well on the corridors and staircases.
- Students do not wear their uniform with pride.
- Classroom furniture is not fit for purpose; displays are neglected.
- Teachers do not smile and teach with their classroom doors shut.
- Leaders hurry from one incident to another, caught in the headlights. Morale is poor.

The good news is that it is rare to visit a school with these features today. When you do, it stands out from the norm.

Take a hard, fresh look at your own school environment each day, with senior colleagues and site managers. Ensure it's the best it can be.

77. LIVING WITH GREY

New headteachers often observe how at deputy level things seemed to be black and white – while as a headteacher, the ultimate referee, certain matters suddenly became greyer.

Some decisions and decision-making processes are relatively clear-cut, while others take more finessing. Strongly held views either side of an argument need to be heard, and there may well be no ready answer which unites opinions.

There is a tyranny sometimes in *either/or* rather than *and/and*. Experienced leaders recognise this and learn to live with grey in a wider social climate that frequently insists on certainty, right or wrong.

'Uniting all differences intact' is how many canny leaders see the best outcomes.

The art of the deal is where altruism and self-interest collide.

78. LEADER AS SERVANT

The great traditions of the British Civil Service – exported across the globe – are self-evidently about service. And service of a non-political kind: civil servants advise, Ministers decide.

In many scriptures, there is mention of the true leader being the true servant.

Self-aware school leaders skilfully face both ways.

They pride themselves on setting the direction and culture within which colleagues work. Equally, they see themselves as serving the professional needs of staff and the personal and academic needs of students and children.

You establish your own ways of doing, as both leader and servant, importantly a style with which you are at ease.

79. SEEK ALLIANCES

Today's educational landscape, in the UK and internationally, is one of alliances, partnerships and families of schools. It is rare to find a school as an island, and the school is usually the poorer for it.

Smart leaders identify where alliances are best harnessed for enhancing the education of their own students. Equally, they recognise that by giving to other schools the wider system benefits.

In loose or tight partnerships, schools compete, share, respect differences. Equity matters. A shared culture of aspiration is imperative.

Seek out a trusted colleague within or beyond your partnership whom you can turn to for wise counsel – call or email them when you are uncertain; send a letter in draft for comment; rehearse some ideas before you present them to staff. Professional associations are an additional valuable resource – use them.

There really is no need to feel alone as a leader.

80. THE CHAIR IS (ALMOST) ALWAYS RIGHT

In the splendid British tradition of the public services, school governing boards comprise a group of enthusiastic lay people representing different aspects of the local community.

Leaders, over time, get the governing boards they deserve. That is, they shape them, they ensure the recruitment of high calibre governors with strong ambitions for the school. A board culture is created which is characterised by private critique and public loyalty – collective responsibility takes time and work to embed. When this isn't working, headteachers have headaches.

School leaders know that their positive working relationship with the board Chair is fundamental to the well-being of the governing body and the school. The Chair is (almost) always right – and may well have appointed you!

Effective school leaders harness the talents and power of their governing bodies to enrich the school community and promote its successes.

TAKE A BREAK

Thank you

Irish supermarket retailer Fergal Quinn, on a visit to the US, wanted to check out a fellow chain's claim to be the 'friendliest supermarket'.

The chain promised that if the check-out staff didn't say 'thank you', then the customer could claim a dollar.

At the check-out, with a few items in his shopping basket, the promised 'thank you' was not forthcoming.

Exuding Irish charm, he asked for his dollar, only to be told by the check-out girl, 'Oh! That promotion finished last month!'

81. EXCELLENCE IS A HABIT

Excellence is never an accident. It is always the result of high intention, sincere effort, and intelligent execution. It represents the wise choice of many alternatives. Choice, not chance, determines your destiny.

Greek philosopher Aristotle

Aristotle's analysis is practical and aspirational. In schools where excellence is a habit, their work is rooted in:

High intention: leaders and teams at all levels set out high, specific ambitions in their respective domains.

Sincere effort: all staff approach their daily and weekly tasks with a sincerity and commitment that is personally and professionally satisfying.

Intelligent execution: all staff think intelligently and practically about the best ways to achieve their goals, whether as administrators or teachers maximising students' progress and achievements.

The best schools *practise being excellent*: their leaders, their teachers, their students.

82. THE TEAM

The team's the thing. Check out Olson's geese!

When you look around the school, where do you take real pride in what is happening? It will surely be where teams, small and large, are working collaboratively with a strong sense of focus.

Effective teams don't just materialise. They need deliberate leadership and willing followership. They need time to bond and finely crafted organisational systems around which they can unite. They require a keen sense of purpose.

School leaders frequently reach for comparisons with and inspiration from the world of sport. There are certainly parallels to be had.

You will distil your own thinking about how best to create and coach teams – and get the best out of them. No school is better than the quality of its teachers – or rather its teams of teachers.

83. CONFIDENTIALITY

What's your definition of confidentiality? Think carefully for a moment. Is it a definition you, your senior team and lead secretaries share?

One dictionary says 'the state of keeping or being kept secret or private'. So which is it – secret or private?

One colleague affirms that in practice in schools confidentiality means 'telling one person at a time' ... 'I confide in you'.

The reality is that the varied interpretation of the word leads all too often to trust breaking down amongst colleagues. Hurt ensues.

As a leader, set out your working definition through transparent custom and practice. Thus trust is established over time, and folk will forgive when there is an accidental breach.

84. NAME FIVE

- A student comes to you and says that all of Year 12 are taking soft drugs.

- A parent comes to you and says that all the parents of children in the infants school are unhappy about lunchtime arrangements.

- A member of staff comes to you and says that no one is happy with the new car parking arrangements.

In each case, you say: 'Name five individuals who have said this.'

Those who have spoken to you pause. 'Well', they say, 'it's not everyone'. You ask them to be more specific. They find that difficult.

It's a time honoured strategy for getting to the heart of a complaint.

Take complaints seriously, but quickly secure a sense of perspective.

85. ARRIVING AT MEETINGS

The effectiveness or otherwise of a formal meeting is determined by what comes *before*, what happens *during*, and what comes *after*.

You'll have your own tried and tested way of drafting agendas, and circulating them in good time. Don't allow AOB – it reflects a contributor's lack of preparedness and can easily drag a meeting beyond its scheduled finish time. Instead, put 'Unintended Consequences' as the final item – invite short reflections on any decision that has been made. What did we not anticipate?

Those expected to present a paper have been well briefed about purpose and length. The agenda is timed and has no more than 5 – 7 items. Seating arrangements and refreshments are smoothly organised.

Crucially, it is clear to everyone attending which parts of the business are to transfer information, which invite discussion, and which need a decision or resolution – unless the chair steers otherwise.

I worked in one international context where the weekly meeting *was* the agenda, the agenda *was* the weekly meeting. Topics emerged by group consensus. Try a meeting in that cultural style – it's illuminating.

86. BEING AT MEETINGS

What kind of meeting is this?

The 'Wagner meeting' – of epic length.
The 'mushroom meeting' – appears suddenly, multiplies rapidly, keeps people in the dark
The 'Stonehenge meeting' – it's been a fixture for ages but nobody knows why.*

If you are chairing the meeting colleagues will look to you to begin promptly, keep to the timed agenda, allow discussion as appropriate, sum up as required. There is no recommended style: be inclusive, confident, clear – and listen keenly.

If you are a participant, what have you arrived at the meeting hoping to get out of it? When do you choose to speak, listen, disagree, debate, comment? Timing is important with interventions.

Nothing undermines a meeting more than a lack of agreement as to why it's happening. Yet despite the regularly heard mantra of 'not another bloody meeting', there is no substitute for bringing together colleagues to share ideas and enhance one another's thinking.

Spirited meetings can make a difference. Creative tensions not infrequently lead to fine decision making.

With acknowledgements to David Pearl.

87. LEAVING MEETINGS

If as a school leader you could make everyone feel at the end of the meeting that it was time well spent – you'd be a rare leader. It's worth asking around your various teams for examples of best practice in running meetings.

What follows afterwards is what makes colleagues feel a meeting has been useful or useless, though it's rare for any meeting to be a complete failure.

Well written Minutes of the meeting are key: the person charged with writing them has the power to take forward new ideas, an important decision or resolution – or cause them to stumble.

Experienced leaders read carefully the draft of Minutes before they are distributed.

When next your Google Calendar pings, don't sigh – learn to love meetings by making them better.

88. MARGINAL GAINS

The language of marginal gains has entered the management world from performance improvements in cycling. Historically in the sports arena, winners have always reached to the very edge of the rule book to gain that very tiny advantage.

Mercedes Formula 1 team boss Otto Wolff speaks of 'prevailing scepticism' in his relentless pursuit of grand prix victories: a deliberate restlessness amongst his team of doctors, dieticians, mechanics, engineers to make the driver and the car go that fraction faster.

Whatever language you use, that virtuous circle of constant development characterises schools where ambitious leadership looks forensically – and with integrity – at how to improve the environment, conditions of service and opportunities for students and staff.

Seize the moment – and the possible marginal gain.

89. THE WHALE PRINCIPLE

If you come up and spout, expect some harpoons.

On occasions in leadership, you have to say some unpopular and unpalatable things. Steel yourself! You may have:

- a case of professional incompetence to deal with
- to issue redundancy notices
- uncovered financial impropriety
- discovered a non-disclosed conviction
- to announce changes to working conditions
- to escort an employee off the premises
- a contested student exclusion.

In these cases, you will want to rehearse your words with senior colleagues, protecting confidences as appropriate. Whatever you do, follow procedures assiduously, properly minuted.

Or, you may just have something a little easier: a difficult staff meeting where harpoons come at you from a number of quarters.

You'll have prepared your arguments well, given yourself a back door, showed an unfailingly positive and professional attitude – and agreed to think further and resolve matters anon.

90. PERSPECTIVE

The school leader is better placed than any member of staff to put everyday matters into perspective.

By the very nature of their work and studies, staff and students are caught up in the minutiae – trying to do their best and sometimes struggling when things aren't going as they want them to.

You are in a different place. You are the school community's lead ambassador, standing back just a little, nonetheless feeling deeply the triumphs and disasters.

No training course or manual prepares you for it. When personal tragedy (death, life-changing injuries) hits a child or a member of staff, it is you who is called upon to offer appropriate perspectives.

And, by common consent amongst school leaders, such events tax leadership qualities like nothing else.

TAKE A BREAK

Parents' questions: a guide

1. Do I believe my child is almost perfect?

2. Do I like rules and regulations until my child breaks them?

3. Am I happy gossiping about the school to anyone who will listen, but reluctant to talk to the head?

4. Do I go in at the deep end when someone criticises my child?

5. Am I an expert because I went to school myself?

If the answer to any of the above is 'yes', please find another school.

6. Am I prepared to work with the school and pull my weight?

7. Can I strike a balance between being a Velcro parent and a ghost?

8. Can I support my child and support the school through difficult times?

9. Can I suppress my frustrated ambitions and let my child be herself?

10. Will I deflect rumour and find out the facts from the school?

If the answer to any one of questions 6 – 10 is 'yes', welcome. We will be able to work with you and your child will flourish.

With acknowledgements to Tony Little.

91. HEAD, HAND, HEART

A number of schools root their curriculum in an approach which ensures that all students access learning which calls upon their heads, their hands and their hearts.

Some leadership teams favour a similar model, ensuring that the heads, hands and hearts of staff are harnessed to provide a rounded education for students. Thus, the intellectual and the academic thrive; the physical and the kinaesthetic are promoted; emotional health and well-being are prized.

In leading a successful school there is no one-size-fits-all recipe. But those which sustain success have thought through what motivates teachers to enjoy their daily workload.

In an era in which issues of recruitment and retention dominate, the distinctive head-hand-heart equation is worth exploration.

Ask yourself: what's special about being able to teach at *this* school?

92. AI BECKONS

The extraordinary becomes the commonplace – at a faster and faster rate. Like the frog which slowly boils in the pan, realising too late that it is cooked, schools risk society's new technologies eluding them.

This decade will see health services transformed by AI (artificial intelligence) and Big Data. What of schools? Facial and voice recognition as a feature of everyday organisation and practice?

The Z generation students who are with us now live actual and virtual lives intertwined. Their social media habits and views on the climate-challenged world are set to impact significantly on how the adults lead.

Forward-looking leaders will set aside time with staff, students and governors to reflect on the lifestyles, technologies and everyday practices of their schools. Schools are conservative organisations in the best conserving traditions. They are also crucibles of change, powered by the young generation.

The problem with the almost tangible future is that the lead-in times are a killer.

93. THE THIRD EYE

The notion of 'the third eye' has existed in mythologies deep into history and across world cultures. Many writers have explored just what it might mean to have a third eye, differently all-seeing and all-knowing.

Applied to school leadership, the third eye is the one which tries to see everyday occurrences differently – and leads to challenging orthodoxies, if only to find out why some things are orthodox.

Great businesses, in order to flourish rather than just survive, question what they are doing even and especially when they are doing very well. They question custom and practice.

Try applying the third eye to your own organisation. Invite a friend who is not in education to assist you. Worth the occasional diversion.

94. PRACTICE SHAPES POLICY

You may already have had the experience – it may be one which awaits you.

A Minister of State from the Department for Education visits you to say that 'we hear you are doing interesting things' in relation to bilingual education/vocational training/teaching of writing/outdoor learning/special needs – you name it.

The accompanying special advisers and civil servants take notes – the next you know your practice has assumed national policy status.

This is a reminder that practice shapes policy, not the other way round. You may be doing something special today in your school which will later find national resonance.

Prepare as best you can for the Ministerial visit. It may well come!

95. CARE MORE THAN OTHERS THINK IS WISE

There's a theme running through this and the following three reflections: it is that the very best leaders challenge the accepted way things are done – and contest new space, beyond what most people think is achievable. They may be engineers, doctors, explorers, architects or school leaders.

The best leaders care deeply about their own vocation. They are passionate exponents of the noble art of teaching and the pivotal role of schools in society.

They believe that caring – in the real sense – for the lives of the young people who are in their charge is vital in today's often fractured society.

These leaders care too about the work-life balance of the teachers who inspire the young minds. They plan accordingly.

Have you ever been told that you care too much about your job as a school leader? Not if you keep into balance your own personal and professional commitments.

96. RISK MORE THAN OTHERS THINK IS SAFE

Proven school leaders take measured risks. They believe that challenging orthodoxies and accepted assumptions is often the way to get the very best out of staff and students.

'Do you really think you should do that?' comes the cautious voice.

'Yes, I believe there is a way to ensure these children succeed where others think they will fail,' replies the ambitious leader.

Taking risks is not being blind to failure. It's about working within and just beyond your comfort areas, occupying different spaces.

You cannot sustain high risk at all times – but at the right points, you show winningly that risk can make a real difference.

97. DREAM MORE THAN OTHERS THINK IS PRACTICAL

Leaders in many contexts dream that a project can be realised when all around them share doubts. These women and men have an unshakeable conviction that a certain vision can be realised.

They call upon all their experience, resilience and key supporters to plan and execute something which many gainsayers thought was just not practical.

On these magic shores children at play are for ever beaching their coracles. We too have been there; we can still hear the sound of the surf, though we shall land no more.

J.M Barrie's magic words from Peter Pan conjure up a powerful image of childhood, enjoyed by children and championed by adults. School leaders who dream such dreams achieve more than many thought was practical.

98. EXPECT MORE THAN OTHERS THINK IS POSSIBLE

We are used to hearing in education about the power of high expectations – rightly so.

Sadly it can be the case that one person's articulated 'high expectations' are really not that ambitious. They have fallen into the trap – maybe unwittingly, maybe through knowing no differently – of 'what can you expect from these children?'

The very best leaders have an unassailable belief that all young people can master a skill or a subject if effectively taught. Indeed, certain cultures accept no other position in regard to the achievements of their children.

School leaders who expect more than others (including some teachers and parents) think is possible very often deliver outcomes in languages, mathematics, the arts, the sciences that leave observers speechless.

Reflecting on these four complementary sections (95 – 98)....where do you stand?

99. WHY SHOULD ANYONE BE LED BY YOU?

Answers on a postcard!

Have you thought about this question? Don't be modest – make a list of those qualities and skills which you demonstrate daily and add up to being the successful leader you are.

Try the exercise with members of your close senior team, individually and collectively. You might identify a skills, knowledge or style gap that shapes the next appointment when a vacancy arises.

Remind yourself from time to time of the reasons you became a leader – and why you continue to be good at it.

Humanity. Clarity. Courage. The essentials of leadership.

100. GRAVEYARDS ARE FULL OF INDISPENSABLE PEOPLE

Whether in government, public, private, faith, non-denominational, international schools – the best amongst the leaders stay resolutely focused on the children and students they serve.

Equally, they are highly skilled in identifying the next generation of leaders. They coach colleagues, deliberately. They sow the seeds of their own redundancy.

Succession planning informs their everyday working: nudging potential future leaders to follow their own instincts, to believe in their own potential, to carve out ways of doing which challenge prevailing orthodoxies.

Today's agile school leader remembers UK Prime Minister David Cameron's parting parliamentary words: 'I was the future once'.

101. ROOM 101

I taught in a central London comprehensive in the 1980s at the height of the IRA's bombing campaigns. The distinguished headteacher told me years later after she had retired that during those years she received by phone daily bomb threats.

She evacuated the 1700 children and 150 staff onto the Westminster streets on some occasions – but not all. Her judgement and nerve thankfully held. That has always counted for me as fearless leadership. Some might not condone her actions, but that would be to misunderstand the times.

There are many contemporary voices who speak and write of *fearless* leadership – running schools without fear of failure. That mindset certainly has its merits.

In George Orwell's novel *1984*, the basement torture chamber in the Ministry of Love is Room 101. In the room, the prisoner is subject to her or his own worst nightmare, fear or phobia.

Fiction of course….but what is most to be feared in school leadership?

Perhaps it is those decisions, having to be taken quickly, which affect all students and staff – and you'll be 'damned if you do, damned if you don't'.

For example, what to do when…?

1. A fifth of the staff, belonging to a particular professional association, say they are joining a two-day national strike.
2. Heavy snow falls during the morning, and a quarter of your students come by bus from neighbouring villages.
3. You receive an anonymous phone call saying school meals have been spiked.
4. There are suddenly two cases of meningitis in the sixth form.
5. A violent intruder is spotted in your school grounds.
6. You are subject to a ransomware attack.

You might in advance, and on the day:

- Rehearse your response to such events with senior colleagues in and beyond your school.

- Run your plans past trusted governors/trustees.

- Draft appropriate email/text/letter communications to students and parents – ready on file.

- Trust in your clear and timely decision, with a clear conscience.

- Read the next page!

TAKE A BREAK

Faith

Two frogs lived on a dairy farm and fell into a churn of milk.

The sides were too steep for them to climb out, and after swimming around for some time, one of them gave up the struggle and drowned.

The other worked his feet to the rhythm of 'With Allah's help, with Allah's help'.

In the morning, he was discovered exceedingly tired but perched safely on a mound of soft butter.

Yes, in the end, it's all a question of faith.

SIX SHORT ESSAYS FOR DISCUSSION

These essays were first published at www.blinks.education

Postcard from Shanghai

Wake up in the morning
Stretch your arms towards the sun
Say something in Chinese
And go to Paris......
Every minute, somewhere in the world there is morning
Somewhere, people stretch their arms towards the sun
They speak new languages, fly from Cairo to Warsaw
They smile and drink coffee together.

Anastasia Baburova

Away from its gridlocked, elevated highways the largest city in the world works. Shanghai: a modern, socialist, international metropolis.

Contrast frenetic New York, chaotic Mumbai, the bedlam of Cairo – Shanghai hums with purpose. Twenty-six million souls occupy countless high-rise towers cheek by jowl with the stylish housing and municipal legacies of the French, British and American Concessions. The Huang Pu river bends through the downtown like a proverbial dragon's tongue.

Bicycles of all descriptions, electric scooters, trams, cars, buses, pedestrians rub along politely. While 'partageons la route' is a vain exhortation sign in France, here it is practised unfailingly. No horns, no red-light jumping, no unpleasant jostling for road space – just simple courtesies.

Spring in Shanghai reveals handsome boulevards bright with luscious cherry blossom. Parks and lakesides fill with walkers, card-players, early morning and evening Tai Chi groups, grandparents match-making their grandchildren. By night, the competing colours of the iconic tall towers, neon adverts and laser beams illuminate the Pudong skyline.

The foods on offer from China's diverse provinces are eye and mouth-watering, served up in enticingly named restaurants. Lost Heaven features Yunnan cuisine; Crystal Jade specializes in Cantonese dim sum; Guoyuan has super spicy Hunan dishes on the menu. All this is an increasingly cashless society. Even the few street beggars can accept a contribution through WeChat the ubiquitous, multipurpose messaging app.

Shanghai hums to the tune of a global future, rooted in a colourful history of welcoming peoples from anywhere and everywhere.

Like Russian dolls, new cities rise up annually within the megalopolis, each larger than a combined Birmingham, Manchester and Leeds. I visit four schools in the new urban developments to glimpse China's dazzling educational frontiers.

Where once the Chinese middle class sent their children to famous boarding schools in the UK and US, now those distinguished brands have come East, spawning hundreds of local for-profit and not-for-profit competitors. To meet the demands of the exponential growth in international and bicultural schools, Shanghai and Bejing alone need an additional 100,000 English speaking teachers over the coming decade.

The medium of instruction in lessons alternates between English and Chinese, frequently blending the two: humbling bilingualism at work and play. The country's thoughts, culture and traditions properly lie in the core curriculum, just as they do in India and Arabia.

A student-led assembly invites teachers to share extracts from their favourite books in English and Chinese. The Principal is welcomed to the microphone to present a few prestigious awards won by students in recent pan-Asia competitions. In turn he challenges students to speak 'English only' on the corridors in the run up to the exam season. British and American English compete for students' head-spaces. The anglophile, bilingual Head of Maths tells me she speaks fluent Chinglish and demonstrates in style.

Cambridge IGCSE reigns supreme in these impressive schools where student attainment is high, where IB scores are at their global best, where the students are MIT, Yale, Zurich and Oxford bound. I reflect on the political mugging of IGCSE in England.

And Shanghai Mathematics is self-evidently in operation here, a reminder that context is everything, that a curriculum model cannot be readily imported in the way naïve UK politicians have contested.

In another school I encounter The Brain and The Oxygen Bar, attractive airy spaces for independent study. A number of classrooms have smart sofas and bean bags in part of the room, enjoyed by small groups of senior students to peer mark essays and plan oral presentations. QR codes are posted on doors for students to offer feedback to teachers and BYD (bring your own device) is embedded practice.

The co-curricular programme in a fourth school takes your breath away. Recent months have welcomed a world-class harpist, an international choir, national poets and artists of distinction. British leaders are pioneering an innovative, bilingual 'head, hand, heart' curriculum, fusing the best of Western and Eastern cultures for the 2 – 18 age range. And tasty lunch menus are something else: stirfried baby cabbage, pickle and egg soup, sautéed duck fillet and pepper.

The education market booms like a Californian gold rush. Entrepreneurs are in their element, Supermarkets proclaim Kumon Math, Saturday schools, tutoring agencies, university crammers. Education, anywhere and everywhere, is the investment the current generation makes in the next. In Shanghai there is no mistaking that imperative.

Teeming, urban China – through its young people – thoughtfully, optimistically modernizing without Westernising. The long march of the Silk Road continues.

Roy Blatchford, April 2019.

♦ ♦ ♦

It's the curriculum, stupid!

Bill Clinton's successful 1992 presidential campaign slogan memorably read 'It'sthe economy, stupid'. His lead strategist James Carville hung a sign with thesewords in the Little Rock campaign headquarters: what was intended for an internal audience rapidly became the election signature tune.

In the contemporary schools landscape, Her Majesty's Chief Inspector has hung up the sign: 'It's the curriculum, stupid'.

Over the years the inspectorate has waxed and waned in its enthusiasm for the curriculum. For teachers at the sharp end of leading curriculum development in schools, Ofsted was in my view at its descriptive, enabling best in the **2009** framework, defining an outstanding curriculum as follows:

The school's curriculum provides memorable experiences and rich opportunities for high-quality learning and wider personal development and well-being. The school may be at the forefront of successful, innovative curriculum design in some areas. A curriculum with overall breadth and balance provides pupils with their full entitlement and is customised to meet the changing needs of individuals and groups. There are highly tailored programmes for a wide range of pupils with different needs.

This narrative happily reminds us at that a school's curriculum is the sum of many parts, including the national curriculum.

In the **2012** inspection framework, there was little prescription; rather a focus on educational outcomes, however schools chose to achieve them. Inspectors worked with a relatively loose yet comprehensive description:

A broad and balanced curriculum which meets the needs of all pupils, enables all pupils to achieve their full educational potential and make progress in their learning, and promotes their good behaviour and safety and their spiritual, moral, social and cultural development.

In the **2018** framework, the word 'curriculum' does not appear as a key word in any of the section or chapter headings. Rather it features as one modestly, yet trenchantly worded aspect among many to be inspected under leadership and management:

The broad and balanced curriculum inspires pupils to learn. The range of subjects and courses helps pupils acquire knowledge, understanding and skills in all aspects of their education, including the humanities and linguistic, mathematical, scientific, technical, social, physical and artistic learning. (Outstanding)

What does the 2019 Ofsted inspection framework say about the curriculum?

It says a great deal. And signals a number of inspectorate priorities which will inevitably lead to intended and unintended consequences in schools. Just watch the growth in 'cultural capital' resources.

The 2019 framework places curriculum *intent, implementation* and *impact* centre stage in its assessment of the quality of education a school provides. The extensive text dedicated to the curriculum certainly marks a departure from previous Ofsted frameworks, and will doubtless generate much fruitful debate in staff rooms about *what* is taught and *why*.

And the inspection framework is quite possibly the first of any globally not to have 'teaching & learning' as a key heading – a significant departure.

HMCI Amanda Spielman clearly wishes the curriculum to be her legacy. Unambiguously, she has commented:

Schools need to have a strong relationship with knowledge, particularly around what they want their pupils to know and know how to do. However, school leaders should recognise and understand that this does not mean that the curriculum should be formed from isolated chunks of knowledge, identified as necessary for passing a test. A rich web of knowledge is what provides the capacity for pupils to learn even more and develop their understanding.

All schools will feel confident that they can embed a rich web of knowledge at the heart of innovative, engaging and powerful curriculum models. In reading in the 2019 framework that 'schools taking radically different approaches to the curriculum will be judged fairly', it is to be hoped that leaders will not be afraid to structure and deliver content that best suits their individual school contexts.

The ambitions of leaders to 'do differently' – for example, in relation to government EBacc targets or the teaching of reading – will need to be matched by intelligent inspection that recognises school autonomy and those individual contexts.

The times are propitious for an energising and intellectually stimulating debate on what lies at the learning heart of every primary and secondary classroom.

Roy Blatchford, May 2019.

◆ ◆ ◆

End of academic year reflection

This past year I have visited nearly 50 schools in the UK and overseas. Sometimes it has been as a reviewer (*Blink*), sometimes as a leadership coach, sometimes to work with students and teachers, sometimes to listen to headteachers' views on a range of educational matters.

I thank them all for sharing their classrooms, ideas and opinions.

One particular visit stands out – to a school where *Work Hard, Be Nice, No Excuses* is a simple mantra lived by everyone in the building. After the visit, I wrote the following letter.

Dear Headteacher and Staff

The quality of education
The College continues to provide an excellent quality of education for all its students, rooted in an open Christian ethos and a simple set of ubiquitous guidelines: *Work Hard, Be Nice, No Excuses.* Clarity of purpose pervades.

ES is a happy, harmonious, intelligent school, at ease with itself, where staff and students share common goals. Teachers and support staff know the students as individuals and thus are able to meet consistently their wide range of learning needs. Students' progress is excellent, with some especially strong sixth-form performances in recent years; teachers continue to strive to raise students' attainment levels at GCSE.

The College's leadership team is highly skilled and restless to improve. They interrogate and fine-tune current routines; they think through carefully any changes they are making and communicate effectively with their colleagues. The way in which middle leaders are being supported and challenged by a 'visiting expert' is typical of the College's deliberate practices. Another example is the way in which leaders are visiting other schools to look at ways in which underachievement with certain groups of students can be tackled more successfully.

The campus presents as very well cared for, and recent refurbishments have enhanced provision in a number of ways. The attractive and busy library sits at the heart of the College; facilities for SEND and inclusion give the message that all students are valued. Classrooms for practical and academic subjects project a strong learning culture through well prepared resources, interesting wall displays and appropriate furniture configuration. The day-to-day use of information technology by staff and students is impressive.

The main hall, with its colourful array of flags from the 50+ nations represented by staff and students, continues to embody all that the College stands for; and the excellent dining arrangements remain another indicator of the fine attention to detail which is characteristic of so much of SE's everyday practice.

The College's meticulous systems and high expectations were singularly in evidence throughout the day of the review: major GCSE examinations were taking place; a Year Group literacy session was being held; cover was needed because of external visits; and Ramadan meant adjusted timings of the school day. Throughout all this, there was no sense of raggedness or time being wasted. To the contrary: in observing 20+ lessons students were constantly on task and teachers were working assiduously to ensure good academic progress.

Students, families, staff and governors can be rightly proud of what is being achieved every day at ES. The College has clearly enhanced its reputation in recent years, evident in increased applications at Year 7 and Year 12. The leadership's ability and aptitude to sustain excellence, whilst at the same time questing wisely to improve, signal a continuing bright future as a 'stand out' local community academy.

Roy Blatchford, July 2019.

◆ ◆ ◆

PISA in purdah

With politicians on doorsteps and civil servants in purdah, this month's publication of PISA* results has not been accompanied by the usual idle chatter around rising and falling standards.

OECD's PISA tests have been running since 2000. They measure the ability of 15 year-olds to apply their skills and knowledge to real life problem-solving in reading, maths and science.

The rankings are based on samples of pupils in each country, with about 600,000 pupils having taken this round of tests.

In the latest league table – based on results for the tests taken in 2018 – China, Singapore, Macau and Hong Kong continue to lead maths and reading rankings. In science the same countries dominate, with Estonia rising to join the top table. Canada and Finland are up there too, as they have been for a number of years.

As to the UK:
- in reading, the UK is 14th, up from 22nd in the previous tests three years ago
- in science, the UK is 14th, up from 15th
- in maths, the UK is 18th, up from 27th.

These figures are based on a sample of about 14,000 pupils in 460 schools.

If government and opposition politicians were to be speaking on these results, claims and counter-claims would doubtless be made for the impact of phonics and mastery maths, academies and increased funding in classrooms.

A more sober analysis lies with Andreas Schleicher, the OECD's education director, who said there were 'positive signals' from the UK's results which showed 'modest improvements'. He went on to say that at the current rate of progress it would take a 'very long time' for the UK to catch up with the highest achieving countries.

So what is the UK not doing that the 'top table' are?

I met recently a group of undergraduates studying education at the University of Reading. Many come from the countries which feature at the top of the PISA league. They argue strongly that culture trumps systems, that the esteem in which the teacher is held in their societies is *the* determining factor alongside the value placed on education by parents. Tutoring outside school also plays a part they suggested.

These undergrads spoke eloquently about the expectations which *all* teachers have that *all* children will succeed. Mixed-ability classes are the norm, as they are in Estonia. The results from China are calculated from just four of its provinces with a combined population of 180 million. Even the most deprived 10% of pupils in these provinces had better results than the average for the UK.

The reasons to be cheerful about our own education system are that many, many children and young people succeed academically and enjoy school, though OECD in a linked survey observed that UK teenagers were found to have among the lowest levels of 'life satisfaction'.

Do we take from all this that the 'long tail of under-achievement' – *the forgotten third* – casts a shadow over UK education that we need to focus on in a fresh, radical, new-look way?

Ask a group of primary headteachers and they say that reducing class sizes would make a significant difference to attainment at 11+. Ask a group of secondary headteachers and they will say that a system of comparable outcomes, which fails a third of students in order that two-thirds can pass, presents a fundamental flaw in our GCSE examination system.

Dig a little deeper into how the 'top table' countries organize things, and examinations at 16+ are a feature of the past when the vast majority of young people are in education and training to at least 18+. Not to mention trusting teachers to assess their own students, externally verified.

And ask folk in Canada or Finland about the balance between school accountability and school support, and they find the Ofsted model (albeit slowly shifting) an alien force.

In summary, we shall not see the UK in the top PISA ranks in the coming decades unless there is a seismic shift in how society values education and teachers.

And in how the profession works with government to challenge the accepted orthodoxy that failure for a third is baked into our system. The Chinese, Japanese, French, Indian, Libyan, etc. undergraduates I spoke to cannot believe we do this. Why would you? Why do we?

* OECD Programme for International Student Assessment (PISA)

Roy Blatchford, December 2019.

♦ ♦ ♦

A New Year's resolution for leaders: prevailing scepticism

A new, predictably unpredictable decade begins. The German poet Goethe wryly observed that everything has been thought of before – the challenge is to think of it again.

For the past several years, my own thinking and writing about excellent schools and colleges around the world has focused on their 'deliberate restlessness'.

Toto Wolff puts this feature differently. He calls it 'prevailing scepticism'. Wolff is the unassuming boss of the Mercedes Formula 1 Team who have won an impressive 87 of the last 118 Grand Prix.

He made his fortune in finance and tech start-ups before investing in Williams F1. He joined Mercedes in 2013 and revels in the ethic of teamwork. He talks of an array of experts that Mercedes has available: mindfulness trainers, nutritionists, doctors and so on. Wolff says he hunts for success in the depths of the human psyche: 'I take the greatest enjoyment and purpose by giving my people an environment where they can thrive'.

School and college leaders frequently reach for comparisons with and inspiration from the world of sport. Matthew Syed is widely known for his book 'Bounce' – and his 10,000 hours of purposeful table tennis practice with friends and a coach in a modest garage, leading later to victories on a world-stage.

'Legacy' by James Kerr interrogates and champions the secrets of the All Blacks and their legendary team spirit. Ed Smith's 'Luck' covers a range of sports and analyses what-ifs, probability and those factors which lie within and beyond the athlete's control. Smith concludes that 'luck is what happens to me that is outside my control'.

Much can be learned by education leaders about marginal gains, strategy and motivation from a wide range of sports. What I find singularly compelling about Wolff's arena is that, as he observes, it takes a team of 200+ dedicated workers to put champion drivers Lewis Hamilton and Valterri Bottas on the track.

As in schools and colleges, it is the Formula 1 back-room staff who are as important as those we watch in awe changing a set of wet tyres in 3.2 seconds. For every Mercedes team member we see in action beside the track in Bahrain or Singapore or Monaco, there are three back at HQ in Brackley. For every computer screen track-side, there are a dozen in the factory.

I have defined excellent schools and colleges as ones which 'deliver superior performance and have a high impact over a sustained period of time'. Amongst the many ways in which they practise 'excellence as standard', these organisations display five special characteristics.

1. There is an unequivocal sense that a 'we' not an 'I' culture prevails.
2. Leaders are very focused on eliminating in-school variation.
3. A never-too-late mentality is coupled with a sense of urgency at the right time.
4. Timely communication of the highest quality pervades.
5. Leaders know that innovation lies both within and outside the organisation.

The Mercedes team's progress and achievements over the past six seasons are rooted in a similar cocktail applied to Formula 1 racing. Just watch this from Ferrari (Mercedes's principal competitor) if you need persuading:

Formula 1 Pit Stops 1950 & Today: youtube.com/watch?v=RRy_73ivcms

So – the New Year resolution is: practise prevailing scepticism. If you practise it already, just touch the professional refresh tab for this new decade.

Further reading

Bounce by Matthew Syed

Legacy by James Kerr

Luck by Ed Smith

Roy Blatchford, January 2020

♦ ♦ ♦

Artificial Intelligence (AI) beckons

The word 'robot' comes from a Czech word robota meaning 'forced labour'. It was first used to denote a fictional humanoid in a 1920 play. By the 1940s Isaac Asimov started popularizing robots and intelligent machines in his great science fiction short stories.

Perhaps it has taken longer than Asimov, George Orwell, Aldous Huxley and Ray Bradbury predicted in their fiction. This decade will surely see robots come of age in the shape of artificial intelligence reshaping diverse aspects of our lives.

- In the arena of climate change, sophisticated software programmes will allow robots to distinguish between biological organisms and pollutants.
- In transport, the autonomous, driverless car is already upon us.
- In home alarm systems, AI can distinguish between occupants and unknown persons.
- In healthcare, robotic surgery assistants will become commonplace.
- In finance, junior accountants are being replaced by AI.
- And 'transhumanism' – the fused human/robot – rightly excites ethical discussions.

What about in education?

The extraordinary becomes the commonplace – at a faster and faster rate. Like the frog which slowly boils in the pan, realising too late that it is cooked, do schools risk society's new technologies eluding them. In too many schools currently, the potential of e-learning is not fully harnessed.

And the GCSE and A Level examination system has barely begun to respond to on-line assessing.

Schools are conservative organisations in the best conserving traditions. They rightly protect the past. At their best, they are also crucibles of change powered by the young.

The Z generation students with us today live actual and virtual lives intertwined. Their social media habits and views on the climate-challenged world are set to impact significantly on how adults lead nationally and internationally.

Forward-looking school leaders are setting aside time now with staff, students and governors to reflect on the lifestyles, technologies and everyday practices of their school communities.

Working groups, comprising learners and teachers of all ages, are studying:

- How to deal effectively with cyber-attacks and ransomware demands – a key safeguarding issue for schools and colleges.
- How best to introduce facial and voice recognition, protecting individual privacy.
- How to introduce 'bring your own device' (BYOD) into schools, so that all students have real-time access, as appropriate, to the world's knowledge.
- How to bring about carbon-neutral school environments, including home to school travel.
- How any part of a school's provision can be enhanced by the presence of intelligent robots.
- How classroom environments can be improved by AI as deployed in healthcare, transport or finance.
- How curriculum content and assessment of students will be created and monitored through AI.

It was another celebrated sci-fi author William Gibson (*Neuromancer*, 1984) who cannily observed that the future is already here, but it's just not very evenly distributed. All of the above – already in place somewhere on the planet – will inevitably arrive on *all* schools' doorsteps. Astute leaders have started their preparations.

When railways were introduced, the questions of the time were: What would happen to the human body at speed? Would passengers faint? If cows saw the red-hot funnels, would they bolt or abort? And now HS2 beckons.

The problem with the almost tangible future is that the lead-in times are a killer. As with the apocryphal frog, schools risk realising too late that they are cooked – marooned in a different age. Optimistically, the students will ensure that their schools and teachers escape that fate.

Roy Blatchford, February 2020

◆ ◆ ◆

OTHER TITLES BY ROY BLATCHFORD

Different Cultures

Values

Reflected Values

Family Guide to Encouraging Young Readers

The Teachers' Standards in the Classroom

The Restless School

Practical Guide to the Headteachers' Standards

Self-Improving Schools

Success Is A Journey

The Primary Curriculum Leader's Handbook

The Secondary Curriculum Leader's Handbook

The Forgotten Third

Roy Blatchford can be contacted via www.blinks.education or at royb88@gmail.com

CPSIA information can be obtained
at www.ICGtesting.com
Printed in the USA
JSHW010353010720
6432JS00005B/8